Mirrors of Astonishment

MIRRORS
of
ASTONISHMENT

Rachel Hadas

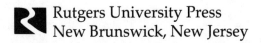
Rutgers University Press
New Brunswick, New Jersey

Library of Congress Cataloging-in-Publication Data

Hadas, Rachel.
    Mirrors of Astonishment / by Rachel Hadas.
       p. cm.
    ISBN 0-8135-1899-7 (cloth) —ISBN 0-8135-1900-4 (pbk.)
    I. Title.
    PS3558.A3116M5 1992
    811'.54—dc20   92-9877
                                                  CIP
British Cataloging-in-Publication information available

To my sister Beth
and in memory of our mother
Elizabeth Chamberlayne Hadas
1915-1992

Contents

Acknowledgments

Some of the poems and poetic sequences collected here have been previously published (either in part or in their entirety, and sometimes under different titles) as follows: "Art," *Literary Review;* "The Bath," *Harvard Advocate;* "A Copy of *Ariel*," *Raritan;* "Cover-Ups," *Ploughshares;* "Cupfuls of Summer" and "On Poetry," *Denver Quarterly;* "In the Middle" and "Visiting the Gypsy," *Threepenny Review;* "Learning to Talk," *Southwest Review;* "Desire iii, v," *Boston Review;* "Love," *Margin;* "An Old Song" and "The Bright Child," *Columbia College Today;* "City and Country (iii)," *Western Humanities Review;* "Genealogies," *Verse;* "Roadblock" and "On Dreams," *Yale Review;* and "116th Street," *Paris Review.*

I am very grateful to the MacDowell Colony, the Ragdale Foundation, and the Virginia Center for the Creative Arts, the places where many of these poems were written. The John Simon Guggenheim Foundation gave me the wonderful gift of the time needed to complete this collection. A Rutgers University Research Council Grant helped with typing expenses.

Warmest thanks also to Jane Churchman and John Heuston.

Mirrors of Astonishment

ONE

Art

i

Translucent etymologies
elbow each other in sleep,
news of the world that lasts
because it never was.
A weedy wind proclaims more rain is coming.
Drought and wet's binary boxes
fit into the same squares that coffin
William Vaughn Moody, Trumbull Stickney.
Half remembered poets from their haloed
obscurities rising, falling
either way cheat the oubliette.

ii

Letters and syllables popping up, so many
spats from a hissing griddle,
squiggles crosshatching a sketch of the possible,
flypaper stuck with a season's stock of phrases?
Add more water to the metaphor.
Say more with less. Use only
ingredients fresh from the garden.
Take the careful colors of the palette
and dab with caution,
ignoring the smear of gold
that daily stains the window.

iii

The rocks that make this house's
foundations once were gold.
Higher and higher the giants piled it,
wheelbarrows stacked with loot,
bulky sack on sack
covering (waist, breast, forehead)
the goddess of earth and youth.
Only the crown of her head,
a feathery wisp, still gleams.
And now she sinks beneath the golden stones
on which we built our house.

iv

To fall asleep in lamplight
and everything makes sense.
The casket labelled "Open Sesame"
waited for its three guesses;
the knot of fruit and flowers
carved on the sideboard gleamed,
each leaf and cluster, with dour ingrained wit.
A sudden snake uncoiling from the casket
answered the riddle right and poured itself
scornfully away across the water,
away from the rich suburb's pale pastels.

v

Ghosts walk here. The divinity student in the guest room
sensed the crowd of phantoms right away—
not that she knew the names, the history,
but dreams and screams so stuccoed into silence!
Too dark to sleep. Too quiet and too dark.
Even the false dawn of a tiptoed-to
refrigerator would never work. The dog
would snarl, the sick woman
stir in her stitched sleep.
Sealed, the house cups its occupants
all in one damp palm of stale affections.

vi

Week-long immersion in gabble!
Charm, exhort, wheedle,
orate, hover, pounce, staccato-stab.
It calls for sabbath, for sabbatical,
some ritual distilling of the actual.
For solid blocks, as bright
and robbable as jewels,
diamond sharp and hard past accident,
tucked into the pattern of daily time divided,
the illness and the cure and the reaction.
Year in, year out, the struggle with one's means.

3

vii

Get to the woman and write her words down now,
at once, before the cold comes.
Summer here lasts eight days.
Each of us is a reservoir of texts.
One by one we'll disappear.
No one will be left to talk to.
Dying fables circle
over the withered tundra
sniffing out pluckable stuff,
ruminating slower, slower, slower.
Dialects wither and dry up like moss.

viii

Smile, dirt of a world
turned inside out. We two
crossed on the winding stair,
you mounting, one hand on the banister,
leading your leashed terrier with the other,
I bouncing down to buy milk, see the sun.
Nods are exchanged, we do not speak. We both
long for trees and grass, even in sleep.
This much kinship I assume whenever
our paths converge on the winding
stair, beloved neighbor.

ix

We shared a popsicle, not cream or sherbet
but big black cherries embedded whole in ice.
We said *Good bye, I'll miss you* with our mouths full.
Your first poem-letter went astray,
went home to you, its tail between its legs,
before it reached me here in timeless space
or codeless time. Yesterday's meager ration
of sun the baby (that word won't do much longer)
squandered on the discovery of wild
strawberries. Ecstasy! Anxiety!
Red-handed, smear-mouthed, lurching through the
  meadow.

x

Skirting the coast, we spotted something black
too far off to be sure exactly what—
two poets trying furiously to flee
the musty usages of our surroundings
and find the radiant messages the sea
surely reserved for our blind inmost eye.
O sky's unchanging azure,
O virginal white sand
and behind it line of tall blue-green
trees that cradle in their somber foliage
what dead and dreadful thing?

Tracing a chiasmus when they praised
a blond flame glowing in the green of June,
the boychild who meant summer growing tall,
my lines connected two new lines, two new
Jonathans. One is running over the grass,
one was put to rest not far from here
when the ground thawed—late April, early May.
Shakespeare wrote "eternal lines to time."
Particular and universal,
elegy, artifact, intrusion:
nothing to do but join the dots I saw.

Cover-Ups

i

Impeccable softness
powders the upturned face
of what a meadow meant.
Weighed boughs: a load slides down.
Muffled squeak. A child's
cheek soft beyond belief
takes shape beneath my palm,
whereupon my whole enormous body
cups to a hand whose fingers tease the nap,
stroke it to dullness, coax it smooth again.
Huge hollowed lap, I ache to cradle absence.

ii

Summer field where many seasons back
we lay and learned each other in the heat:
revisiting the place, unblemished snow.
The field was never there.
Vistas of tumbled whiteness:
relentless winter pulls the bedclothes up.

iii

I knew that I would squirrel away the snow,
save it in the space between my eyes
and only later put to use
that tiny tract of saturated white,
burnish some dull hour to a high shine.

iv

Trodden by daily traffic, little feet,
the rug wears thinner and a hole appears.
I spy the hole and worry at its edges
and itch to pluck it like an instrument
and pick at it, a wound,
press it, peel the scab off,
pull aside the curtain,
touch what's underneath.

v

Cartouches of exposure and invasion:
hieroglyphics violated children
obedient to universal law
draw of their bodies: arrows
press inward to black holes
outlined in angry red.

vi

The wound, he called it, women really are,
between their legs, where their life is.
However that was hedged with irony,
it's woman/wound that has remained with me
and underneath the bandage
a woman's voice apostrophizing silence,
embroidering it like a special cloth
taken from a cabinet, shaken out
only occasionally, to be spread
over a festive table
or a marriage bed.

8

vii

A gesture of revelation
strips off the crumpled linen
so nakedness emerges from its cave,
oppositions melted at white heat,
cliffs and promontories draped in white,
barely recognizable, a scroll unrolling,
soundless as a frozen waterfall.

On Poetry

i   Lyric

All possible excrescences lopped off,
its essence must remain
austerely crystalline. True lyric should
exclude all trivia. Thus Critic X

objects to Proust's including
the lift-boy's sister shitting in the back
seats of hired cabs as "mere detail
that must have struck the master as worth noting

but seems to us obtrusively grotesque."
Poppycock. Proust wasn't writing lyric.
The creel he hauled up groaned with what he both
found and invented, all equally fresh,

salty, shiny with imagination.
The epic gates of ivory and horn
may as well open wide for defecation
as eating, sex, or sleep.

Homer's horizon accommodates heroes
who drink wine, piss on the beach, weep at sundown,
go to bed with braceleted boys or women
and every dawn the sun comes up again.

But lyric's narrow confines
ought to tighten, tighten like a migraine.
Small explosions follow, their throbbing
a welcome price for maimed intensity.

ii *Trivia*

By trivia I mean unmediated
worship of nature; the idolatry
of mere delight in an unfolding iris,
a scudding storm cloud, one's own tenderly

remembered hemorrhoid. The language of
all these must be interpreted. No one
ripening apple cups its simple sense.
Take away the apple, keep the fruit's

lingering odor: regret for past
hours spent on hands and knees in search
of strawberries remains, and is enough.
Red-stained knees, mouth, fingers—these are sweeter

in the recalling than subordinated
to each year's petty facts: arthritic knees,
plague of black flies, or a foraging
toddler who ate the berries faster

(devouring time) than you could ever pick them.
See apples turn to strawberries on this
magic palate. Or a smell of onions
and okra frying in olive oil

conjures up a village's bright mornings.
Whole years fit into a tiny window,
sunny, untouchable, distant,
the scene it frames an idol out of nature.

iii *Nature*

Hardest of all. Is it whatever fails
to stick out, a sore thumb,
from its surroundings, or just what we're used to,
or something no human hand has touched?

"Papa Bear hammers nails into the roof,"
whoever wrote the version my son reads
felt the need to add to *Goldilocks.*
Homo Faber twiddles his thumbs for want

of natural work. Nature as order asks
constant attention; nature as wildness, neglect.
Though Wesley Ward's junked cars offend my sense
of order and of nature, year by year

they're masked by higher grass and growing trees,
will vanish soon (I hope) like Ozymandias . . .
The books piled on my table
are also unnatural, messy, hard to dispose of

in their small way. Itself a pied creation,
poetry explores a middle ground,
one foot stuck in a rusty pick-up truck,
one hand shading the eyes against

sun, moon, stars—whatever natural light
we see our earthly lives in.
Not one but two lights, and a single urgent
finger pointing—is it up or down?

12

City and Country

i   The Retreat

Ah, the conspiratorial
ganglia of this city,
its macedoine of clues,
its plethora of uses.

Why did the barber smile
when J and I passed by fighting?
Why does the vegetable lady
have a blue bruise over her lip?

Must every passer-by,
must every casual spy,
every sentient eye
you happen to encounter

embody something huge as history?
Overwhelmed by data,
we punctually scuttle
each summer to the country

or seashore's blessed blankness.
Portentous tigers may
stalk the dusty garden,
may pace the stony beach,

but they do not accost us.
They hardly seem to see us.
No mirroring accusing
eyes peer from trees or water.

Our reflections here
have to be self-sufficient.
Or you could say we leave
to see the city and to be unseen.

ii   *The Dream of Divesting*

When it's finally time to go away,
how much of myself shall I shed?
Happy the empty suitcase;
happier the empty head.

Deliciously divested,
I open the door of the house
only to find what was a farm
is now a grandiose

opera hall. Rehearsing
"La ci darem," I wear
nothing but sheer soprano;
the rest is all thin air.

The summer dream of stripping
has come true, then? Not yet.
These are the words I'm singing
in the dream duet:
Take off my nightgown,
let my hair fall down,

put a crown of stars upon me;
wrap me in myth,
let desire with
its purple fire clothe me.

Absolute nudity
is a deluded hope.
The very air I'm singing
is woven trope on trope,

a tissue of rich figures
we are condemned to wear
as long as we're condemned
to breathe the air

of city or of country.
Forever greener grass
is cleverly reflected
in memory's glass.

iii   *At a Distance*

We eat our daily bread but we don't taste it.
Familiarity doesn't breed contempt;
it fosters an invisibility

so thorough that to remember anything
we have to have recourse to elegy.
Take this June in the country.

Lilacs, fireplace, barn,
meadow, rainbow, anniversary—
all tempered with nostalgia's deepest green.

Our crude attention happily responds
to what is unintelligible still,
utterly new and strange as an infant's squall.

Tirelessly then we work to recreate
the primal moment, building little shrines
tagged for convenient reference:

"This we did here, remember?"
I do remember. Generous attempts
doomed because they're hopelessly belated.

The magic has leaked out of the foundation.
The imitation bed's made up, the table
spread, the lilacs faithfully perform;

we see the season; eat and sleep and dream.
In the city we dream of the country.
In the country we dream of a country

always anterior and always distant.
Distance is the only magic key.
Distance is the aphrodisiac.

Except for the golden child asleep between us,
everything—including you and me—
looks better at a distance.

This is being written in the country.

Cupfuls of Summer

i

After the great divide, the slope's round bone
rises each summer in its maple mane.
Wind in the leaves rings changes, and the light
pleats patterns every hour. Neon-bright
tall rushes show where solid pastureland
goes gooey underfoot. I had to dare,
when I was small, to walk as far as there
and see our house's dark side like the moon.

Later the way to reach sublimity
or get a little closer to the sky
was climbing up above the white-pine line
(it wasn't timber) to a quartz-flecked wall
on a bare hilltop. Domed, medieval,
heaven clasped and capped the compass like a crown.

Last year I hardly found the way back down.
The field's stern contours had been ruffled, smeared
in aspen, chokecherry, juniper, sumac,
making the change less stark than I had feared,
but only the old magnet drew me back.

ii

The rhythm here is not so much recurrence
as slow accumulation. Things stand still
and using them we measure how we've grown.
Who last came here a child no longer sleeps alone.
Upstairs winter-stiffened mirrors swell
and stir with shoulders, hair, a rapid glance.

The past made more palpable and put away
labelled in drawers or simply left to lie
is instantly available. A crowd
of revenants can separately recover
the treasure that was buried years ago
they have returned a decade or more later
in order to be able to discover.

A silence in which absences loomed loud
crashes and washes, only to recede
and leave the same old dust under the bed.
In every room, however hard the years have scoured,
a layer of decorum has endured,
hard to get off as honey once it's spread.

iii

The memory custodian guides them over the grounds.

What Rilke called the homelessness of things
here pauses and takes stock and folds its wings.
A single answer to the many questions
renews itself each summer without strain
as all the flowers gaping in a garden
draw strength from one deep rain.

The lumpy little hills give out a word.
Unspelled, unspoken, not in any book,
it chirps like crickets, passes like a cloud.
The air is rinsed with silence till it's heard.

Late August: no mythology but apples.
Each tree a world. The world is made of trees.
To taste a bite of every galaxy
one would eat nothing else, and still it can't be done.

Voices out of nowhere lose their terror.
Distant as dogbarks floating over water,
they are pronouncing an invisibly
hovering love they say will reach us later.

iv

The sky today is watermarked with faint
connections I keep trying to recall.
This fading catscratch: pale red dotted line
between the squares where day and night are twin.
A sinewy yellow tomcat sidles out and in
before I've really looked at him at all.

And what the dream-cat cannily foretold—
a wordless stitching of opposing realms
together? Nothing ventured, nothing gained
or even aimed at—just the way a paw
pushed a pipecleaner over a wooden floor
in the wan light of early morning rain.

How could plain catflesh manage such a taut
cohesion? Continents of grey and white
float in her fur, iceberg-mysterious.

Deep, sore, and tiny as a paper cut,
the sliver I discover between sleep
and each day's field—one world laid on another.
Those dream instructions cobbled it together.

V

The vision came near Sheffield. Circling hills
turned to a ring embossed with textured gold.
Late night filled up the valley like a cup.
Some thirsty giant might have snatched it up
and sucked the rainbow clean—oh yes, there was
a rainbow, running down into the grass,
stubby and salmon-radiant. It came last.

First we cried "Look! the light!" No time to waste:
we all dashed out onto the soaking lawn,
reached with a single gesture, found the one
whose hand we wanted, or some recognition,
and having touched were mostly quiet. (B.
dived for his camera.) "Catch the color! See,
the gold's gone rose, the rose is turning blue!"

See Spot run! The only thing to do
was bounce for jubilation in the grass
(the dog did that) or stand and use our eyes.

The precious vintage gathered drop by drop
of purest light—we stood around the cup.

vi

The central stone on which successive waves
battered and broke, the figure at the altar
has powers that are perennial, so profound
that no one knows why they keep coming back
long after the first crop is underground.
Roots ramify. An altar of the dead
under the lawn protects and is protected.

One cloudy August evening, a man
faces me, holding something in his hand—
racquet, mallet, scepter, bough, or wand.
Now young, now tall, now bearded, and now old,
is this my husband, brother, son, or father?
A slant of light cuts through the piles of cloud
and seals my eyes a second and it doesn't matter.

When a deep crust is pierced, the waters break,
cautiously seep at first, then rush and flood
the living layer beneath each summer's feet.
Racquets held high, we're running toward the net,
crushing the bones this instant. They smell sweet.

TWO

The Mirror

Paradise: first the world within the mirror
and then the knowledge that the mirror mother
and father faithfully
would render back the world and never waver
or crack. So that the lesson
of the broken world
needs to be taught remedially to us
big oafs who saw ourselves
in surfaces that never seemed to tremble.
Visions from which they scrupulously shaded
our infant eyes light up
belatedly. The atmosphere
we bathed our little lids in
dries; unfamiliar absences take shape
and death's black hole. But wait,
absence is the other side of love.
All of us, confronting—sooner, later—
some version of the mirror
recognize our faces cracked with age
suspended in solution for our children
to find themselves within our steady gaze.

Expression

Our faces peeled to raw banality
       of flesh and bone
seem to say nothing looked at one by one,
convey so little that we gladly don
       cheeks, lips. The mask of flesh
fits each soul's uniqueness with a face
molded by selfhood to expression.

I used to be so certain. From the skull
issued an inimitable voice
       singing its quintessential
       tune. And each eye's shade
of green, grey, brown was like a forest glade
       whose pine or maple tree
was captured by, reflected in the soul
       as colors are laid on

by a skilled painter. Physiognomy
       in every architectural
       flourish and least detail
I knew was eloquent of the ineffable
inner stuff- call it spirit, self, or soul.
Words are debased coinage; pass them by.
Gauge a person by a flashing eye,
       a lip's significant curl.

Because we none of us possess a mirror,
    I stubbornly persisted
    in this romantic error,
aspiring to interpret self from skin,
until a snapshot rudely showed me the
    extent to which the soul,
immune to wishes, to idolatry,
    remains illegible.

Mother and toddler ride a carousel.
Their faces show no feeling at all.
    Clues to their states of soul
are how she bends; his hands that clutch the pole—
the eloquence of bodies poised in space,
    iconography without a face
because our human masks are far too thick to show
    glimmerings of selves we barely know.

In the Middle

The story of summer is always somehow the story of sleep,
of covering our heads for the sheer pleasure of oblivion,
and the possibility of peeking out.
Why do you want to know about the past?
the sphinx demanded, crossing muscular arms
over her breasts. *What good will it do to know
exactly why or how your father died?*
Yet a child is supposed to answer the elders' questions,
no matter how bloody his two skinned knees,
brimful of grief his heart, raspberries filling his mouth.
*Whose child are you? How did you get to the island?
I don't suppose you walked here on the sea.*
Intricate scaffoldings clambered up backwards,
the voyager swings blind through the great hotel.

Brilliant mornings we pull the covers up,
shut out the sun the better to perceive him.
Radiant he tiptoes in.
The shade pulls shaped like tiny lobster buoys
he tugs, lets light into the dreaming room,
then dives into the middle of the bed
and lies between us, waiting to be born.
I remember my father's warm left and my mother's warm
    right
thigh as I sat between them in some front seat,
sensing myself even then in a not so permanent
crack of creation I would never stop
issuing from, but the place itself was mortal.
Why do you want to know about the past?

A Copy of Ariel

Not only is the same bookmark in "Poppies in October"
But I can smell the mildew still—a seamold's
Rich and acrid pale-brown sour tang.
Or is it that the book enfolds a world
Bleary but flowering with possibilities?
Each morning I gazed at the milky sea
And it was always morning. It was morning
When, making one more effort to efface
The person I had always been, I thought
"Why not translate "Poppies in October"
Into Greek?" And it was also morning
When my first original Greek poem
Was born of gazing. But Plath's poppies first:
I recall those little bloodied skirts,
The thin as paper dry and bloodied lips,
Translucent delicacies, onion skins,
And the skeptical question "*Do* you do no harm?"
(My italics) which could be translated
Rather than answered. As for my own poem,
It never got beyond the first two lines:
"*Phortoma gaidouria kai karpouza!*
Phtasane ta kaik' ap' ta nisa."
(Cargo of donkeys and watermelons!
The fishing boats have arrived from the islands.)

The poem was no more than a transparent
Container for four juicy neuter plurals
(Donkeys, watermelons, caiques, islands)—
An embryonic grammar beyond which
I failed to move. I had no more to say.
No human face looked back at me. A life,
Motives—illegible. What I still can see
Is the horizon, pallid amulet
Beckoning above the shimmer of grey sea;
And sense, even now, my dim determination
To hold onto what could in any case
Never be lost. So that those ghostly poppies
And smell of paper mildewing in mist—
Smell edible, perishable as meat—
Both open vistas, far, symmetrical;
Whereas the donkeys (hoisted with a crane
Onto the old *limani*) or the glistening
Bulbous melons bouncing in the hull,
Naked of meaning but for brilliant outlines,
Were called back into being only through
The rules of grammar and my meager Greek
Wordhoard—called back, though, as genuine
Visions, even if the haze through which they shone
Yielded to each morning's arrow: sun.

Sentimental Education

When my eyes rove in search of recognition,
what fills them, as if they were ears, not eyes,
is nothing I can see, but roaring surf,
its nightly entertainment and announcement
when I lived on the island. All night long
it used to grind an endless message out
and never climb the beach. I used to gaze
blankly as if by staring I could scan
in that white band of sound some rune of future
and not of future only. Present too.
As if by paying close enough attention
I could decipher the illegible
story of my life and what it stood for:
a glass partition only broached in dreams
again erected with each day, again
and always an enigma. And if I
couldn't read the riddle, then who could?
I listened to the waves as if they led
to further signs, to ramifying maps
of passage in a life for me to choose.
Once I knelt down between a rusty tractor
and a puddle of orange water dwindling
on cracked cement under the noon sun
and tried to pray. And once
I heard a kitten's or an infant's mewl
leak from between my twenty-five year-old lips.

There was no other sound,
there was no father left, I had to mother
myself, there were in fact
no instructions past my own nose.
Oh yes, the flaming sunsets; yes, the surf's
portentous growling. But the sea was mute,
the rosy dawns were dumb, the granite mountain.
Turning my back on these would tell no secrets;
but even zero veiled itself from me
until I tore myself away like skin
and walked into the story of the future.

Visiting the Gypsy

A cool May night, green leaves
exuberant against the lamplit rain.
In an unfamiliar part of town
we went to hear the stories of our lives.
How soft and warm the gypsy's hands. And do
we patients put one palm in them, or two?
You, I remember, gave yourself to her
equivocal pink and black
magic right away. I felt held back
(craning from the arm of the single chair)

by the first lesson that the gypsy taught:
to learn your fortune you must pay in coin
you yourself have scooped from deep within.
Without such cash no answers can be bought.
Her lap and hands were soft, but not her eyes.
They probed our faces, weighing truth and lies.
Lovers' confusion. Homesick. Pregnancy
desired, difficult. People envy you.
You smile but you are torn between these two
men. Someone's giving you the Evil Eye.

All this I write as if it were declared,
oracular; but rather it was fished,
questioningly. We answered as we wished,
you more, I less. Our mysteries were shared—
that, as I see it retroactively,
presented her with our one certainty.
Secret disappointment with your lot.
Anger. You're nice to people but they're not
nice to you back. Some person in your house
loves to give orders. I see nervousness.

Whoever claimed this dirty linen could
wear it (what's the proverb?). Separate
lifelines, loves, and histories were old hat.
But for one evening that we somehow should
merge into one; that we could, skittish, peer
through the gypsy's window; sit in her
overstuffed chair; could trust her with a hand—
that was the true adventure for us two,
that was the spell that both of us could brew.
Her Delphic lines took two to understand.

We deconstructed generalities
no feeble human creature could deny.
All of us suffer from the Evil Eye.
What seemed to one of us obscurities
the other would decipher. You don't see
that other people envy you? That he
is the man who takes but never gives?
We each found means to reassure the other:
She said a change was coming to your lives!
The gypsy watched us, silent as my mother.

Her plateglass window boasted painted hands
at prayer. Behind it were arranged two packs
of cards, tarot and ordinary; wax
candles; several statuettes on stands;
old incense; knives; a spoon; a purple book;
cigarettes; herbs. A passer-by could look
in at our threesome's archetypal scene,
cartoon of fortune-telling ritual,
with the new wrinkle that here was a twin
client who proffered her four palms for tall

tales, for cliché and mystery and fable,
for human aspirations scaled to size.
For us to sift, as best we both were able,
her farrago of guesses, truths, and lies.
Out into the green evening, and on
our way—henceforth as sisters of the palm,
bound by the power of an unwritten tongue?
The first time that I saw a caravan,
in Corfu, I turned to my companion,
knowing no Greek. I gestured; said *tzigánes?*—

the ancient language ringing through me like a gong.

Learning to Talk

Some of the ways my parents passed me language
or I just took it: Mother's groaning platter
of pristine etymologies
glossily displayed and known by heart
somehow without ever being sullied;
Grandfather's journal during his engagement
("Showed B. my sonnet. She asked why it only
had fourteen lines"); my father's putative
unfinished novel of the Occupation
in Athens (lost? or merely from the first
a dreamwork?); my elder sister's private
diary secretly filched and read
by the same reprehensible young person
whose son at not quite three corrected her,
me, I mean, fussily, for calling something
red when it was "actually orange."

None of us was afraid to put a name
to anything; but neither did we lift
our faces from the pages of our books.
And our insinuating pedantry,
nibbling at an utterance's edge
still adheres: the way we picked up words,
more or less gently licked them into shape
like Vergil's verses, sent them gingerly
out into the inscrutable great world.
Periphrases, lacunae, and corrections;
the cunning madman's fixed hyperbole;
the squishy diction of gentility—
what talents, what avoidances, what losses!

Roadblock

Call me the bee buzzing in the museum.
The younger sister fussing through a house
still stiff with loss.
The meddling goblin in the mausoleum.

My dream: with three in the front seat, we drive
under a bridge—and halt. A huge grey bus
blocks the whole road, including us,
the only travellers who are left alive.

It's drizzling; the windshield wiper blades
busily gesture, yet we're nearly blind.
You two seem not to mind
blank windows, pulled-down shades.

I mind. I want to get out and explore,
to move around
the deathly obstacle. "Don't make a sound,"
you say. (Who are you?) "Don't go near that door."

Our mountain drive last month—that wasn't dreamed.
We three again. We ran a dog down. I
alone looked back, alone let out a cry.
I saw it lying in its blood and screamed.

So tell me what these images portend.
Am I a noisy bird of evil omen
or just a person, apprehensive, human,
moving ahead, kid sister into woman,
stonewalled by death each time she rounds a bend?

116th Street

I walk downhill and lean into the wind.
It is and isn't the first time. Hour, weather
errand all proclaim Now and Again.
Late comes the sense that all will go on without us,

late the undoing. When it's all undone,
still winter sunset bleeds across the sky
coldly unfurling alpha and omega,
ending and origin. The wall of winter

still stands behind the mists
of our preoccupation,
still lingers in our speech.
Patterns of thought run deep.

Late comes the sense we're carried by a stream
that has worn grooves in the ground already.
Was it pure illusion, sensing each
impulse and gesture as spontaneous, new?

And all the while we were ourselves ideas,
not new ones, either, of if not a mind
call it a system. An intelligence?
Buffeted by gales blowing up from the river

(when I was ten years old they blew me back
up this same hill, yet then I felt autonomous),
belatedly I take it in as law
that it is time to lean into the wind,

assume personae without irony.
Today—not today only—loyal daughter,
term I construe now in a wintry way.
No sooner have I grasped this than I come

face to face with yet another rune
blown in my flinching face (or are they one?):
laws we thought we had enacted turn,
chisel in hand, and carve us like a stone.

The Bath

I have been floating in the mild hot tea
of sisterly concern for my exhaustion,
my nature's frantic spattering and splashing.
Long immersion in the herbal bath
steaming with sage and camomiley smells
steeps me in Greece. We only
choose half the memories into which to lower
an aching body and forget awhile
the press of gravity. Choose half, half choose:
we cannot choose them all.
We cannot choose which faces
insatiably to gaze at.
So with the kindly brew of her remembrance:
savoring its warmth even as I sense it cooling,
I lie back down, I brace myself against
my childhood. Present, future like two rings
I carefully take off and lay aside.

Genealogies

The Muses are the daughters of Memory.
Family resemblances flash out at moments
when the reminiscent voice begins
either to crack under the weight of feeling
or to lift off as lyric, winging, soaring
at once toward knowledge and away from facts.
It turns its back on the familiar,
strains after still unformulated questions
if a voice can have a back to turn.
But who can doubt intelligence is bodied?
What's miscalled inspiration merely means
the daughters take dictation from the mystic
mother; fish treasures from a well so empty
that at the bottom gravel gleams like mica,
flickering forms that mock the seeker's eye.

Flickering forms that mock the seeker's eye
and come from where? Jealously Memory
guards her stockpile till the daughters turn
to less demanding tasks, then overwhelms them.
They have no choice: to turn the treasure down
means to lose it. So, obedient
although still abstracted, they remember.
The law of anamnesis reenacted
over and over blurs the boundaries
of learning, inspiration, recollection.
I turned to you, a flower to the sun.
The shadowed face as what to love and also
a way of loving was your legacy.
Later I ventured on a variation:
turning my own dream-heavy head away.

Turning my own dream-heavy head away,
I sped along the parallel and found
solitude in the island of my body.
Mirrors of astonishment, water, trees
spoke through the window of my meditation,
truer than human voices in their weaving
between the phases, inattention giving
way to thirst, or hunger to abundance.
You never taught me how to make a choice,
or make a friend, or how to think of endings.
How to exclude. That choosing means exclusion.
A task I had to come to on my own,
you never taught me how to tell the truth.
Setting things down came second. First you taught me—
slow pupil, I'm still learning—how to read.

Slow pupil, I'm still learning how to read.
Reading is a refinement, a digestion
of those crude texts which in their turn revise
the endless rough drafts of experience.
Unearthing words renews connections where
something had sifted numbly to the bottom,
broken in the trench, the careless diggers
shouldering their shovels, stomping off to lunch.
Some small bridge existed, even so:
hence Auden's Caliban refers to the
restored relation, not the new-created.
Creation's sheer raw heat is what confounds.
The rest is polish, wear and tear, reworking—
all the tasks of recollection's children.
And I am one, and you are recollection.

And I am one, and you are Recollection,
the double parent with whose many lives
I briefly coincided. Brevity
that once was spiked with elegy appears
natural now as shadows passing over
obedient to a law. Obedient
and even calm between impatiences,
I fumble at the rudder, steer my life,
peering for omens in the winking cistern
or turning to the sky. Miasmas rise
steadily from calendar and mirror.
Habit disperses them; they thin like smoke,
there but invisible. Father, I age
and turn to you as I would turn a page.
The Muses are the daughters of Memory.

THREE

Desire

i

Winter in the city. Molten cold.
Towers of darkness, piled precariously,
teeter at the soiled century's verge.
River and sea, confounding poisons, spill
and sully all the waters of the world.
From this beast's dull belly watch me conjure
against the blackness of the winter river
a hill of heat, a castle built on air.
Selfish, the dreamer's mirror,
moonlight serenely glinting over no
expanse but pure attention,
and ice breaks, water bleeds,
tiniest waves begin
to ripple, pulse, dissolve into desire.

ii

Vivid pictures of
bodies at their old play
take me by surprise,
come close enough to touch.

Here we sit.
Between us is the fire.
A log breaks and you look
up. Our glances lock.

Magical again, the space between
two bodies poised and taut
because we will not act upon the thought
of silken sense reeled out
like a bright tightrope, I was going to say,
slicing the room in two.

But no such thing—
rather a ribbon functionaries snip
inaugurating some new era I
and you don't hanker for.
The ribbon's barely visible, the room
lit by the gleaming remnants of a fire.

iii

Hymettus honey blue
falling away beneath me, faster, faster,
I skim the top and tumble over sky
to tidal foam, abandoned
outpost of memory, past or still to come,
husband, son
marooned in a tumble of land and water

and rise, and ride,
straddle the bony hourglass,
subdue the dumb dimension,
knock the smirking idol
off its pedestal
and flailing free
swoop down into the honey of that sea.

48

iv

Syzygy: planets lined
up against the sun
so spring tides tug at us, and the new moon.

Absence is a rooted gravity
drawing me inside and deep and down.
I miss my son.

The wings that hoist me out
of the maternal self,
that flap against habit, tenderness, rage—

these same wings shape the cage
I sink into and sleep,
carapace I am home

in most when I am dumb.
A skull-eyed shadow
sees herself and smiles

in a black window. Silent
at the turn of the exhausted year
the planets burn.

V

Tracking the virgin snow with rosy soles,
a wolfskin over his shoulder,
little cupid swaggers through the dark.
He holds a bowl of flame.

Knowledge enormous makes a god of me?
Desire enormous shrinks me back to baby.
Tiny seeds of fire
sink in the snow, and what will sprout next spring?

Deep-seated fever. The original
germ once planted, nemesis supplies
belated ailments for a single hour
of dissolution at the blushing hearth.

Let fictive borders melt in crimson heat,
vanish under snow: there's no escape.
An hour is too much.
Boundaries, molten, frozen, realign,

waver from ice to icon,
finally congeal as absence.
I teeter at a glassy platform's edge.
A locomotive roars to its red destination.

vi

A darkened room. Fanged icicles shine through
the moonlit window, glimmering pale blue.
The hearth's hot emanations shudder red.
Lines of hot and cold bisect the bed,
fleshing the bones of absence in the night.
Borders dissolve and swim back into sight.

Over a gleaming field, long lines are scratched
invisibly on whiteness, snow crosshatched
to labyrinth in whose daedalian strands
enchanted, helpless we hold out our hands.
Moonlight makes these faint engravings gleam
greyly: with dawn they vanish like a dream.

Each dreamer here, ensconced in cell or tower,
must shape an invocation to the power
that weaves so many semblances of place
into one web and fades without a trace.
Startled proximity fluently invents
fresh formulae for ancient lineaments

of language, as that yes, a name is real.
Emotion's not a word for what I feel
but tangible as ice or ash or fire.
The snow is mapped with arrows of desire
pointing us toward one another's bright
beacons of recognition in the night.

Astonishing how opposites are true.
Light isn't dark, in out, I am not you,
man is not woman. Even as I trace
the boundaries, I ache to stroke a face,
the features spelling out what I have found.
Wait: something bigger trembles underground.

Subterranean blazes, long restrained,
channeled, tunneled, all their heat contained,
rumble and stir. Extinguished embers flare
as buried fire begins to scent the air
and strain toward the border it will breach,
exploding silence with a burst like speech.

vii

Daily negotiating half-thawed channels,
how habited, how clothed I had become!
Freeze this icon: in a moonstruck room
lit by a single candle like a cave
I stand by the fire wearing red and black,
blackfigure warrior, one hip thrust out,
and take my shirt off: how you bend to the
snow of my breasts against the fire's heat,
shaping your responses to the act
in the improvisation of the dance
as two performers whom a pantomime
enables to approach the molten center
of a dumbshow whose mirrorings entwine
icicle and volcano into one.

viii

In the mirror of your absence I see my face
and turn away from firelight's nonchalance.
A gesture of affection is bestowed but not accepted.
When I die I want to be remembered with curiosity,
a richly written scroll unrolled partway.
Jeweled snowdrifts gleam and do not answer.
As one who hurriedly leaves the house on an urgent
    errand
and loses herself in tracklessness of snow,
azure allurements fashioned out of ice,
smoke spiralling blue signals against sunset,
and flies from wish to fear and back again
and circles in the forest until twilight
and slides in the dark across a frozen firepond
glinting in moonlight like an iron weapon
and comes back home and drains a cup of wine,
spicy, crimson, while a fire of branches
crackles its red calligraphy on snow
and celebrates the burning strip of red
under the cave's black door, and accepts gifts
piled, like ice, like jewels, on a salver
scorching with stored-up heat,
so appetite to appetite catches fire,
flames leaping high and sparring with the dark
and sinking down so soon we have to hurry,
I must hand you the sweet gift quickly,
it must be warm. The bird of paradise
ripping apart his cage in masculine
destructiveness turns out to have been preparing
a nest for the egg she furtively has laid.

An arm is stretched out, luminous in firelight
for the imagination's orange heat.
Cold gems shaken, snowflakes from wet fur,
fall to the ground and hiss and disappear
as you loll in the blaze of my memory
on a soft blanket of snow
I ache to lay my cheek against, but black
floods the windows and the wish sinks back
sucking under for another wave
to rise and break in pain. I touch your hair,
in the dance of thought you move away from me
off toward the mountains of your southern kingdom.
I lie and let desire ramify
into a phantasmagoria: blood
spilled on snow, a floor stained blue, then strewn
with icons of remembrance and regret,
starless sky, eyes of a newborn, velvet
presences flooding the kaleidoscope
with color in the courage of my death.
In the absence of your mirror I see my face.

ix

Syzygy: tidal siphoning of blood
from an arm outstretched, vulnerable in sleep,
its liquor thinned to ruby. The tall flood
of ocean smashes boundaries, the sea-
wall crumbles under the invasion: deep,
deeper than any barricades that border
the waking world. We thought it had to be
one house and garden tidied into order,
but rushing water overwhelms that dry
idea—soup in which familiar fish
perform strange evolutions: a third eye,
a quirky fin—presages of new
species of seeing? Waters break the wish
to read the dream, the floodtide washing true.

x

In the dead eye and target of the winter,
colorless flatness all along the sky.
So I unlatched the greenhouse and stepped in.
Emerald vines abruptly ramified
under beds, over boxes, twining room
to room. Blood thickened: bricks
of dull caked river ice, now thawed, now crazed.
The current running January slow,
lights flickered in the city's theater.
What I was turning into the boy saw,
pointing to my vagina under water:
More babies there? And I said *No, not one.*
Only the moon's dumb flood along the floor.
Head down, I hurried home and slammed the door.

Tamped in that tower now,
what stubborn contradictions to unravel,
a devil's bargain. Irresistible
to yank away from what was long ago
settled upon, the chairs and tables so
sunken into one posture as to seem
immovable. Yet banished bubbles do
finally rise, there is an undertow,
the empty hive flaps loosely, and the river
silts up with choking amber,
the honey-heavy dowry, nuptial treasure,
smears its glistening cargo on the water,
two lives' impedimenta lashed together
with tendrils tough as cables that no one
can disentangle now. As in a dream
the aged couple years have crusted over
feebly wave; are borne away downstream.

xi

In solitude, in waves that break like grief,
livid flashes light lost hours up.
Strenuous instants reenact the body.
I re-rehearse your magical ascension.
Somersaultingly the appetite
lands on its feet as love and is off and running.
I pursue panting: Come here! I need to name you!
Love turns a young bewildered face to me,
eyes wide, lips parted; we back up a pace.
The bridge of glances spans a rainbow's reach
from the original mirror of the eye.
Yes, you were mine from the beginning. Not
mine only—far from that! I mean my creature,
my infant phoenix curled inside the fire.
We do not ask a child for love; we feed him.
Rooting, wriggling, he replies "More! more! "
Question and answer coincide one hour.

Happiness

i

What if I could sit right here forever,
my cooling tea in a mug
hotter and hotter from midsummer sun,
the cat behind me in pine-dappled shade
itself immobile like the afternoon
halted in its sumptuous July blaze?
Would each of my fresh bruises then remain
in its particular stage of blue or green
or yellow, never fading, never healing,
and would the flowers transplanted where I fought
the tall tough bushes whose hard stalks so bruised me
droop forever, never taking root?
The salty trickle underneath my breasts
would still to a rivulet carved in relief
or slow to glacial. Since the merest drop,
they tell us, can wear stone away at last,
so it would wear me, for I would be stone,
stone woman in unending afternoon
at a stone table under a stone sun.

ii

Out of all the amplitude of summer,
permanence's posture: how to choose?
My son, my snuggler, in his lighter sleep
makes sucking sounds—a memory of nursing,
or maybe navigating those new teeth,
or chewing dream-cuds, their texture
light as air yet firm enough to last
through hours of nocturnal rumination.
Awake, absorbed, all senses satisfied,
when he's being read to, for example,
while also licking something undemandingly
delicious like a popsicle and maybe
breathing in the pine scent from the hammock,
all the while clutching his elephant and lambskin
now hallowed for six years,
he emits little creaks or groans of pleasure,
unvoiced, unconscious. And would I freeze that?
Would I freeze us three
mother son father triple parallel
horizontal in the early mornings
smuggling the cargo of our consciousness
across the blurry boundary between
the worlds of sleep and waking?
Would we stall forever
in a drowsy hinterland?

iii

Already in the pineshade
shadows have sharpened somehow, and the cat
has silently shifted position to inspect
a patch of belly, sore, pink, licked to baldness,
diagnosed last summer as "most likely
psychosomatic. Has anything
changed for Morel lately?"
There was the rub. She rubbed it. So do we,
or it rubs us. It rubs us rough and smooth.
Smoothness if repetition gives the illusion
of moving with, moving as fast as change
so change itself becomes invisible;
rough if we struggle, rough if we resist,
and how can we help resisting
the speed at which things move,
or if not speed the stubborn ruthlessness?
Abraded raw, would I still wave a wand
to keep us here immobilized in summer,
or meekly, smoothly glide on into fall?

On Dreams
to C.A.B.

i

Invisible to each of us in turn,
to love and to receive became twin ropes.
Grasp greedily: you'll end up with a burn.
Let go a bit: it slackens and escapes.

Your blue eyes warming like the summer sea,
you envy me? The marriage narrative—
life in the middle, years still left to live—
imprinted both familiarity

and staleness in the deepening of years,
as stains creep slowly through a layer of lace
but still the family tablecloth's in place
and mealtimes happen at appointed hours.

Love's jigsaw complications never rhyme,
their intervals too close or else too far.
Of course we know this is what art is for:
a decorous arrangement, space and time

ordered to be both near and far enough
to see each other clearly now and then
and to envision either kind of end
and still move parallel. So much for love.

ii

Tell me your dream. I know it as a house
beyond whose brick walls no
visible gulls swoop, no possible
sunset is reflected off the water.

I saw the lighted windows.
Then the landscape sighed
and shifted like a sleeper turning over.
No: your dulled lights,

your lips that smiled in pain,
whole landscape that in order to forget
I had first to learn,
drilling to memorize, and then give up.

We had no past, just present.
No present, only future.
Your cancelled future matched my used-up past.
Nothing but this moment in the tunnel,

as if I could brace myself for the coming storm.,
your voice, your presence
pulled away from light
ahead of time. I cannot bear the loss.

iii

The horses of Achilles! I was one.
Fixed to that chariot, pacing toward death,
I traced the path of ending with my back
and turned my head and prophesied in anger.

As one recognizes certain friends
only after passing, over a shoulder,
our fleshly meetings now occur in dreams.
Another life: anterior, not future.

So I leap on the bandwagon of sleep.
You went into the hospital at night
and in the morning nobody was there.
A wind of disappearance chopped the air.

A wooden room next; dais; lavish feasting.
But you were beyond eating, so you said.
And I could not approach you; you kept wishing
to be alone. "All right," I said, "I'll go

and leave you and not write." And you cried, "No!"
This is the writing, long after the fact
of dream inheritance. There was no end:
no graceful way out of the vaulted room.

iv

The beauty and encumbrance of this world
where mild temptations slide out of their depth . . .
Two men at work by floodlight in the dusk:
the driller and the one who holds the lamp.

Everything became a book I read:
your razor blade among the satin pillows;
your mother's sudden velvet-mittened fist;
my own impatience, stumbling at a sigh.

Each day collates its own anthology
whose references bind me to blue air.
Not that this makes a conversation, quite;
more a contemplation of exchange,

minus plus minus, chewing over loss.
As my lost youth, you mourned.
Paralysis and possibility
played out against a blacker scrim than my

generation got to shine upon;
having said which, even the word "my"
gradually comes apart. Again
affection strains its fleshly boundary.

v

FAX me your dream. Or first take this of mine:
long yellow trains of fear moved through the night.
At midnight I got on,
partly for shelter, as one carves a niche

to make a nest for longing, clambered up
onto a high throne, into a bunk bed,
naptime in the mind, the poem frozen.
Outside in the city it's midsummer,

roaring and lurching of a million lunches,
hats and balloons like flowers in the streets,
a hopeless glut of blossoms
crushed against the glass of one more day.

Real life. Was this the foreground? Any hour
looks small and hard, and how should I exchange
my loving gravity, quotidiana
for the unfinished, always rebeginning

plunge and swoop of yet another chance,
brushing of a wing against the sky?
Every hour makes reference to the question
listlessly, dice shaken in the rain.

vi

Poised yourself on a brink,
discoverer of borders underneath,
gentle artificer, how did you come
to lodge inside my heart?

Were you concealed in summer's magic attic
underneath the layers of dust where no
edges poked out but years could twinkle through
the baggage of oblivion like stars?

These stars are valedictory. They consign
silent messages to every dawn
and dawn breaks grey, another day, another
season, the old challenge

looming there like Evil Dream in Homer,
perfidious incubus with false instructions,
not reassuring, not a grandmother
offering plates of food for the new hour.

Oblivion could be alpha and omega,
before and after. Still you could wake up
into the steadfast flower of your body,
the wounded hours, the blank day's eye still open.

Four Poems at the End of Summer

i   The Bright Child

A child's incessant questioning of names,
customs, appearance, history, how things work
(Why is that called a culvert? Why do people
have gravestones when animals don't?
What is music made of?)
abstracts the would-be answerer's attention,
who, though well-meaning and omniscient,
can only choose a single strand to trace
and so leaves hanging
all other objects of this urgent quest.
These cool September mornings, gemmed with mist,
cobwebs glint on the lawn
tiny and scattered. Or are they all one?

ii   Light on the Past

Consider. In the middle of a life
suddenly publicity's immense
flashlight is focussed unremittingly
on whatever surface he presents.
Not surface long. The paper of his age,
already layered, already flecked and stippled,
not by violence, by nothing more
brutal than living, soon begins to crack.
Insert a blade, a fingernail, a file—
the whole facade, once loosened, starts to peel.
Surface? Facade? Everyone needs a face.
But what lies underneath the hanging strips
isn't pretty to the avid gazers.
Under the paper, bats
nested in the hollows of these walls,
their innocent blind wizened
faces have chewed on history,
battened! Stale decisions,
musty leavings rain down from their naked nest.
Complacent, blind, repulsive?
What is revealed cannot again be covered
no matter how completely
the place is scoured, fresh paper pasted on.

iii   Unnamed

Late in the summer of drought
a quiet brimming wells
up. It is kin to rain
that makes the woods and meadows
bloom with mild brown mushrooms.
But it is not rain.
Nor is it the cricket in the corner
telling of shelter; nor the seated forms,
the pharoah forms of massive seated dreams
whose phantoms we hold up.
Or it is more than these:
a brimming and a stillness
not to be further named,
silent in the yellow
slant of the season's passing,
a shape of what has and has not been done.

iv   An Old Song

Monotonous, old-fashioned, sentimental:
I used to feel a little bit ashamed
at twenty of so simple-mindedly
responding to the cycle of the seasons
as what gave rise to poems
that sang the passage of each one in turn:
poems of fall and winter, poems of summer and spring.

I could no more grow tired of this house,
each creaking board, each corner's angled light,
than I could tire of weather, trees, the ocean,
of eating, breathing, sleeping next to you—
occasions, every one of them, of praise
since poetry began. Yet in this lifespan
parts of our earth are beginning to disappear.

Knowledge is left, but dark with elegy.
Late, late we turn to rinsing out the waters
it's crystal clear (belatedly) we never
could tire of. Nor does one tire of memory.
But memory is what comes after,
is never enough, needs poetry to help it,
and even so takes wings the more you want it.

I love you. You and I are vanishing.
Idolatrous at forty, unashamed,
I call out names and praise
to catch and hold what slowly
and not so slowly moves past mortal reach.
Poem and praise wear down to catalogue.
Call it a trellis for our imperfections

to climb on, twine on, finding their own shape,
assuredly impermanent and marred.
Autumn's already rampant in the garden's
tangle of endings I can never tire of
more than I could of me, our son, or you.
Where elegy and reclamation meet,
there is the ground for immemorial song.

Love

Your feet, big, shapely, dirty
(we all go short of water every summer
as if our muck can save the water table)
I focus on as you move off in time
conceived as space, whole homemade landscape you
created, that immediately drew you
helpless within its borders.
Over that line, across the room, beyond
our toes: ray of a gaze
blind with ideas, milky as a river
too bright with mist to see.

ii

Used to each other to the point that we
no longer look to one another's gaze
to see what that could tell us; mirrorlike
it gives us back what we already are.
At least the baby's clear that we are two,
not of a kind. Biology doesn't tell him,
only the greener parent principle.
You go to him, he calls for Mama; me
he asks for Daddy. Even if for us
the grass has gone invisible with use
he sees it. So we keep each other green.

iii

The door clicks shut behind us.
In the quiet, loaded branches stir.
Slowly we pace around the golden orchard.
Years ago you'd flap a hand at me,
imperious, preoccupied, and say
"Sit down. Sit there. Don't talk."
Undone by such authority, I'd sit.
Now as you pick apples up
I bend to touch an aster and remember
the miniature landscapes that I painted
prophetically years back: a walled world.

iv

Smelling like the pair of German shepherds
your brother nightly tussles with in preference,
apparently, to wife or children, you
enveloped me. We wrestled
silently on the tumbled bed, unwashed,
our clothes, half-unpacked, spilling
onto every bit of moonlit floor.
Passion: unlooked-for, inarticulate,
that long fierce gentle meeting
of bodies in the middle of their lives,
lives in the midsummer of our bodies.

v

Or else a rainy morning lets us creep
upstairs to plug our pungent bodies
together, then separate to merely two
mortalities—and all before eleven.
You dreamed last night of skylines codified,
stately rhythms rising from the Hudson,
and the old hell of universities.
Thoughts veiled, I walk, the baby on my back,
and pick him buttercups, a daisy, clover;
peer in at the empty cabin's window.
For Sale. Bed, cupboard, stove; and a piano.

vi

Before first light the cat and her cornered mouse
have woken us: *squeak* and the long deliberate
crunching of little bones gradually counter-
pointed beyond the wall by the baby's soft
wordless hum, not breaking out of quiet
but sleep spun audible, a thread of voice.
Rain-soaked grass drenches my feet, calves, hem
today as sun beats on my back. I bend
to pick wild strawberries invisibly
bedded between their leaves and moss
but warm and scarlet. Some are overripe.

vii

Flesh-colored memories. Plump, bruisable
young bedded body; still life on the wall;
red posters and red bunting draped from windows;
Cambridge, April 1969
shooting out green sparks of strike and spring.
"And strike because they're squeezing
the life out of you . . ." And each squeeze imprints
a plum-blue bruise—those soft
impressionable years! The salmon sheets
suddenly stain scarlet with her blood.
He says, "You're such a woman."

viii

Love as the secret doubling of bodies
under the covers until the crisis birth
yanks them apart—then the long cutting of
the tail by inches. *By inchmeal a disease!*
shrieked Caliban, cursing the only parent
and teacher he had known. Love as, also,
two bodies only superficially one.
It took me years to learn to sleep with you—
real sleep, not euphemism, sinking back
on one another's silence. The centripetal/
centrifugal juggle of two matched affections.

ix

Our visiting relatives, trunk-legged, round-bottomed,
stump off on their walk embracing.
Behind their backs we call them giant redwoods,
not meaning it especially kindly, yet
they love each other just as much as we do,
match as we do: both tall, deliberate,
and infinitely gentle only to each other.
Even our pair of flickering stilettoes
has once or twice been elevated to
the awkward pedestal of an ideal
happiness by others less well matched.

x

I mother you you father me vice versa:
take the exhausted person off, discard
the mom and dadness of who's child, whose child
means less than the warm back we each of us
lie against, the body where we anchor
ourself, the imprint deep as blood. Perpetual
stoas, arcades, and alleys
loom and dwindle, mark our mutual
distance, proceeding down the avenue
clutching a clue, love's puzzle
not yet, not ever done.